D0108801

r

The Bathroom Blunderful Bloopers Book

———— • ————

by

Russ Edwards
&
Jack Kreismer

RED-LETTER PRESS, INC.
Saddle River, New Jersey

THE BATHROOM
BLUNDERFUL BLOOPERS BOOK
ISBN-13: 978-1-60387-089-4
ISBN: 1-60387-089-X

Red-Letter Press, Inc.
P.O. Box 393
Saddle River, NJ 07458

www.Red-LetterPress.com

ACKNOWLEDGMENTS

EDITORIAL:
Jack Kreismer

•

BOOK DESIGN & TYPOGRAPHY:
Jeff Kreismer

•

COVER & INTERIOR ART:
Jeff Godby

•

CONTRIBUTORS:
Kobus Reyneke
Jim Tomlinson
Rory Tomlinson

The
Bathroom
Blunderful
Bloopers
Book

Bottle Cap-italists

When corporations get a shot at a market four times the size of the US, they rush in where wise men fear to tread. The lure of money and the idea that the capitalists can show the commies how it's done is just too much for them to resist. And so it was when China opened her refrigerator doors to western "pop" culture.

Coca Cola brought all its marketing skills to bear on the China market but found that something was lost in translation. "Coca Cola" in Chinese sounds like "Bite the wax tadpole" or, depending on pronunciation, "Female horse stuffed with wax."

When Pepsi cracked the China market, their slogan was "Pepsi brings you back to life!" What the company wasn't aware of was its translation: "Pepsi brings your ancestors back from the dead." All the better then - just that many more to take the Pepsi Challenge.

I think that gay marriage is something that should be between a man and a woman.

-Arnold Schwarznegger

The Buck Shops Here

In LaCrosse, Wisconsin, a sporting goods store's grand opening had an ironic twist. Perhaps not being able to bear the suspense of waiting for the customers to come looking for him, a deer crashed through the store's plate glass window to surprise the hunters in their lair.

The deer scattered customers and rearranged the stock for a while before someone got the idea to throw a tarp over him. Once disoriented and subdued, one of the more macho customers wrestled the buck by its antlers to eject it from the premises, thus taking away the animal's store charging privileges.

Man All Wet

A fellow from Albany, NY, was taken into custody after he jumped into the Hudson River when he spotted cops. The police say he took the dive because he thought he was wanted by the cops. He wasn't.

If you're killed, you've lost a
very important part of your life.

-Brooke Shields

Brass Ackwards

What's an 18-year-old to do when he needs money? Many of us remember making cash by recycling newspapers, cans and deposit bottles when we were kids, but one hapless teen near Albany, New York, didn't have access to any of those. What he had was ammunition and a local foundry which paid money for empty shell casings.

The problem was that he had to fire hundreds of bullets to retrieve the casings but he had no gun.

Necessity may be the mother of invention but in this case she bore a rather backwards child.

The teen decided to place the bullets in a vice and strike the primer with a hammer and screwdriver. The surprising thing is that he got away with it for so long. He had a bucketful of brass before he got a bellyful of lead.

He was rushed to the hospital and survived, but don't make any bets on for how long unless they can find a donor for a common sense transplant.

Oh, by the way, he raked in a sweet $6 on the brass cartridges. Ka-ching!

Bathroom Blooper

It Came from Beneath the Toilet Seat

The Pacific Northwest has its Bigfoot, Scotland has its Loch Ness Monster and Naron, Spain, has Poopacabra. The creature first attacked 30-year-old Iris Castrovered in May 2014, biting her on her bottom while she was using the toilet. The green and yellow snake strikes when it's least expected and even the local men are fearful of this "Jack the Zipper" which travels from house to house using the sewers. Nervous residents have been advised to pour strong bleach down their toilets in an effort to keep the creature at bay.

Lotto Nerve

A British senior citizen (senior subject?) realized her life-long dream when after decades of playing lotto, she bought the winning lottery ticket for the EuroMillions $181 million dollar jackpot.

For decades she had faithfully kept a ledger of the numbers played and so knew full well she had won the fortune. What she didn't know was that her husband had thrown the ticket away. Bet the conversation at the dinner table was frosty that night!

Belgium Waffler

According to a Belgium news agency, a ne'er- do-well in Liege was being questioned by police investigating a jewelry store heist.

Apparently being interrogated by a half-dozen Hercule Poirots all at once proved too much for him. Desperate, he needed an alibi and fast.

He then remembered the old adage "When in doubt, tell the truth," and blurted out the fact that would prove his innocence in the jewel robbery.

He couldn't have robbed the jewels he said, because at the time he was across town robbing a school.

Honesty may be the best policy but as a legal defense, it kind of sucks.

What's Wal-Mart?
Do they sell, like wall stuff?

-Paris Hilton

Phoning It In

Sometimes an extra-smart action causes an equal and opposite extra stupid reaction.

Such was the case when a car thief answered the phone that he had just stolen along with the vehicle.

The caller said that he had seen the ad in the paper and wanted to buy the car at the full asking price and arranged to meet.

In an all-too-human reaction, the dollar signs in the thief's eyes blinded him to any possible danger and he kept the appointment.

There he met the police officer who had baited the trap. The crook got a free ride to the police station while the victim got her car back, losing only two minutes off her wireless plan.

Fiction writing is great.
You can make up almost anything.

-Ivana Trump

Record Mistake

None of us can truly see the future but some of us are spectacularly bad at it.

One man who had a fair sense of things to come was Mike Smith, a heck of a talent scout. That's why, when he saw a band in a small club in Liverpool in 1961, he invited them to London for an audition.

They showed up at the Decca Records studio on New Year's Day, 1962, and played their hearts out.

They went home and waited weeks for an answer.

When it came, their manager Brian Epstein delivered the bad news.

An executive named Dick Rowe had called to say that Decca had passed because they sounded too much like a popular group called The Shadows and that groups were out anyway, especially groups with guitars. And those haircuts!

Just for you youngsters out there who were born only the day before yesterday, that group was the Beatles.

Baptist Blunder

A fiery preacher in Florida was trying to contrast the biblical figures of Peter and John and the walking on water story.

He was stressing the point that Peter stepped out of the boat in faith even though he immediately plunged down into the water. None of the others, including John, even bothered to try.

The preacher enjoyed the rapt attention of the congregation until he asked, "Which would you rather have? A wet Peter or a dry John?"

The rest of the sermon was lost in a sea of giggles.

If It Doesn't Lift, You Must Acquit

A 43-year-old East Chicago, Indiana, man did what we all do from time to time. He got mad at his boss. The next thing he did was more unusual.

Intoxicated, he decided to seek his revenge by making off with his boss' forklift. So began the midwestern version of the OJ chase.

After the police finally managed to pull him over following the low speed chase, he was taken into custody more gassed up than his getaway vehicle.

Surfing the Pipeline

When major storms struck Australia in 2007, the rain turned Brisbane streets into wild and raging torrents. They also inspired a brainstorm in one local lad who thought surfing the inundated streets was a good idea.

He waxed up his board and caught a wave but wound up with more whacks than he counted on. The worst came when his foot got caught in a storm drain and thousands of gallons of runoff flushed him down. The rest was a wild ride through miles of sewers, an experience that could most politely be described as the worst "wipe out" ever.

He was badly battered and beaten when he finally emerged from the sewer system, the nose of his surf board faring much better from the experience than his own.

I don't diet. I just don't eat as much as I'd like to.

-Linda Evangelista

Race Case Goes Off Track

You've heard of the insanity defense and the Twinkie defense but how about the NASCAR defense?

That's what a federal prison inmate tried when he filed a $23 million lawsuit against everybody's favorite sports association where cars go faster and faster around an oval until they crash.

According to the suit, NASCAR influenced the convict to be driving 135 mph. In addition to his tickets, he claimed NASCAR was responsible for his illegally obtained credit cards so that he could attend races and buy officially licensed NASCAR products and beer. Oh, and apparently, while he was enjoying funnel cake, Jeff Gordon's car poisoned him with DuPont chemicals.

On the bright side, when the judge reviewed his NASCAR complaint, he was pretty much assured a speedy trial.

> If Lincoln were alive today,
> he'd roll over in his grave.
>
> -Gerald Ford

Bathroom Blooper

It Wasn't the Razors that were a Bit Dull

It seems that men have always been reluctant to read instructions. The distaste for directions dates back to at least 1902 with the debut of the Gillette Safety Razor. It was reported that hundreds of men were dissatisfied with their shaves and threw the razors away in frustration. Turns out that it wasn't the razors that were dull, it was the men who failed to read the directions to unwrap them first.

Just a Speed Bump on the Information Superhighway

A 26-year-old South Carolina man managed to evade police with some skillful driving during a chase on his motorcycle. He even managed to capture video of the chase.

He was so proud of his driving that he then completely muddied up his clean getaway by posting the video online.

That's when he discovered that he and the police shared a mutual interest in YouTube.

This particular motorcyclist wearing a helmet to protect his brain? Maybe not so important.

Awww G-men

In the early 1960s at the height of the Cold War, with the world teetering on the brink, the Federal Bureau of Investigation, under the direction of the square-jawed, true-blue and ever-vigilant J. Edgar Hoover, manned the ramparts of Liberty, protecting the nation from enemies both foreign and domestic. Communism was the foreign threat; pornography, that malignant tumor on our American way of life, was the menace within.

It was against this tense historical backdrop that the Bureau began one of its most momentous investigations. Not since the days of Elliot Ness and his Untouchables had a federal agency taken on such dark forces of insensate evil.

Finally, after two years of intense investigation, bringing to bear all the agency's resources and manpower, all the very best and the brightest that the United States of America had to offer, the results of the investigation were in and they were stark and disturbing indeed: the lyrics of *Louie Louie* were deemed, officially, "unintelligible."

Banned in Boston

Marketing. It's everywhere nowadays. It's what gets you to buy a certain car, drink a certain soda and use a certain denture cream even though you don't have dentures. Once in a while, however, a marketing campaign can backfire. Such was the case when the Cartoon Network decided to promote a show by placing LED signs all over certain major cities.

Being ads for the Cartoon Network, the style was a bit odd- or advanced- however you'd like to look at it, but it was confusing enough to scare a Boston resident into reporting a terrorist threat.

The subsequent shutdown of the city during the search for bombs was not cheap. It cost the head of the network his job and the company $2 million in reimbursements to the city's emergency response teams.

We have a lot of kids who don't know what work means. They think work is a four-letter word.

-Hillary Clinton

Courtroom Comedy

Lawyers can make a case, if nothing else, that they know how to ask a silly question. Here are some of the more ridiculous ones asked during trials.

• "You were there until the time you left, is that true?"
• "The youngest son, the twenty-year-old, how old is he?"
• "Were you present when your picture was taken?"
• "Were you alone or by yourself?"
• "How many autopsies have you performed on dead people?"
• "Was it you or your younger brother who was killed in the war?"
• "Did he kill you?"
• "You don't know what it was, and you didn't know what it looked like, but can you describe it?"
• "Without saying anything, tell the jury what you did next."
• "How far apart were the vehicles at the time of the collision?"

Every city I go to is an opportunity to paint, whether it's Omaha or Hawaii.

-Tony Bennett

Pill Poppers Meet the Coppers

Where does your family like to shop for drugs? Not that over-counter-kid-stuff but the real deal. The stuff you get from Dr. Happy. In Oklahoma, the Bureau of Narcotics makes it a breeze-one-stop shopping in police station lobbies all over the state.

The stations have drop off bins for prescriptions so people can rid themselves of pills that are outdated or not needed anymore.

One family from the town of Edmond was a little confused as to the exact nuances of the system.

Assuming that the policy was "Take a Benny, Leave a Benny," they went into the stationhouse and helped themselves to the drugs, reaching deep down into the disposal bins up to their armpits. The entire pill-a-palooza was captured on a security camera.

One of the suspects objected to her arrest by complaining that nowhere on the sign did it specifically say that you cannot take anything out.

That argument was just too big a pill for the judge to swallow and so the woman and her entire family were given a healthy dose of justice.

Bathroom Blooper

Fire Down Below

A Florida man was working on an old motorcycle, his pride and joy. He was revving it up on his back patio when suddenly it slipped into gear and crashed through the back door, dragging him along with it. It flew over on its side in the kitchen, spilling gas. His wife called an ambulance and he was taken to the hospital. His injuries relatively minor, he was sent home, but when he saw the state of his house and beloved motorcycle, he went into a deep depression. He sought the comfort and solace of the bathroom where he sat and had a cigarette. What he didn't realize was that his wife had sopped up the gasoline with paper towels and threw them in the toilet. When he put the cigarette butt down between his legs to dispose of it, the toilet exploded. This time, the trip to the hospital wasn't so quick considering the damage to his nether regions. He did learn two valuable lessons that day; smoking cigarettes is dangerous to your health and the only butt that should be anywhere near your toilet is your own.

Third Time's Not a Charm

A bank robber allegedly pulled off a heist at the PNC Bank in Harrisburg, Pennsylvania, not once but twice. The suspect was arrested, however, when he went to the bank for a third time to check his account balance.

Going Postal

Khay Rahnajet, an Iraqi terrorist, built an intricate letter bomb. He carefully armed it and wrapped it so that it would be instantly lethal to its intended victim.

He then took it to the post office where he mailed it off and then went back to his lair to await the news that his enemy was dead.

He waited and waited and waited- so long in fact that he was on to other nefarious schemes.

One day the mail came as he was busy plotting other deaths. Absentmindedly he opened the parcel and ...!

Yep. He neglected to put enough postage on it and it came back marked "Return to Sender."

I've never really wanted to go to Japan, simply because I don't really like eating fish, and I know that's very popular out there in Africa.

-Britney Spears

Church Bulletin Bloopers

Often written in a hurry, amended
at the last moment and bereft of proofreaders,
church bulletins often provide some
funnypage reading for the faithful as seen here.

Thursday at 5:00 pm there will be a meeting of the Little Mothers Club. All ladies wishing to be "Little Mothers" will meet with the Pastor in his study.

•

Ladies, don't forget the rummage sale. It's a chance to get rid of those things not worth keeping around the house. Bring your husbands.

•

This evening at 7 PM there will be a hymn singing in the park across from the Church. Bring a blanket and come prepared to sin.

•

Ladies Bible Study will be held Thursday morning at 10. All ladies are invited to lunch in the Fellowship Hall after the B.S. is done.

Anne was a great girl. Hopefully she would have been a Belieber.

-Justin Bieber, during his visit
to the Anne Frank House

The "Over 60s Choir" will be disbanded for the summer with the thanks of the entire church.

•

A bean supper will be held on Tuesday evening in the church hall. Music will follow.

•

Barbara remains in the hospital and needs blood donors for more transfusions. She is also having trouble sleeping and requests tapes of Pastor Nelson's sermons.

•

The ladies of the church have cast off clothing of every kind. They may be seen in the basement on Friday afternoon.

•

Mrs. Johnson will be entering the hospital this week for testes.

•

This being Easter Sunday, we will ask Mrs. Lewis to come forward and lay an egg on the altar.

•

Low Self-Esteem Support Group will meet Thursday at 7 to 8:30 p.m. Please use the back door.

•

The Associate Minister unveiled the church's new campaign slogan last Sunday: 'I Upped My Pledge - Up Yours.'

Stealing 40 Winks

Across the pond in the jolly olde U.K., police nabbed a burglar who just couldn't manage to stay awake for his getaway.

When police responded to an early morning burglary call, they found the homeowner's car keys stolen as well. They went outside expecting the auto to be long gone, but instead, they found the burglar snoozing behind the wheel.

His rude awakening won him indefinite accommodations at the local bar & breakfast.

Red Planet Costs a Lot of Green

No one can question the smarts of NASA geniuses, but even they can have "duh!" moments.

A team at Lockheed-Martin used English measures while working on a Mars Orbiter in 1999. The rest of the team insisted on being all scientific and stuff and used the metric system. The result: an English-Metric Mutant which was lost in space along with $125 million of NASA's money. And whether you measure it in US dollars or a metric ton of kilobucks, that's a lot of cash to lose.

Resume Rejects

Actual items gleaned from resumes of people
who are probably still looking for work.

• "Wholly responsible for two failed financial institutions."

• "It's best for employers that I not work with people."

• "The company made me a scapegoat, just like my three previous employers."

• "I have an excellent track record, although I am not a horse."

• "My duties included cleaning the restrooms and seating the customers."

• Achievements: "Nominated for prom queen"

• Experience: "Stalking, shipping & receiving"

• Hobbies: "Drugs and girls"

• Skills: "Strong Work Ethic, Attention to Detail, Team Player, Self Motivated, Attention to Detail"

• "Able to say the ABCs backward in under five seconds."

• "Instrumental in ruining entire operation for a Midwest chain store."

• Languages: "Fluent in English. Also I have been heard muttering Gibberish in my sleep."

I made a misstatement and
I stand by all my misstatements.

-Dan Quayle

The French Connection is a Little Too Tight for Comfort

For a proud country like France, the shame must be unbearable. If it's not, it's at least extremely expensive. Seems they just ordered $20 billion worth of trains that won't fit in their train stations. They are just too wide.

They can't return the custom made rolling stock but they can do the next best thing- retrofit all the train stations. They've spent $69 million so far and the cost is likely to balloon into the hundreds of millions. That's a freightload of francs.

Supposedly the national rail operator gave the wrong dimensions to the train company.

Somebody's going to catch it in the caboose for this one!

You mean, like a book?

-Justin Timberlake, when asked what was the best thing he had read all year

Bathroom Blooper

Toilet Paper Pyre

They call it a "rolled house" in Alabama. Most people would refer to it as a house that's been "TPed." When pranksters festooned a home in Dora, Alabama, with toilet paper, efforts to remove it proved catastrophic. Should you ever be faced with the same dilemma, heed well this family's experience and don't use fire. Now to be fair, they didn't light the paper on the house straightaway. They lit a tree draped with paper. Just about then, a breeze came along and blew the flaming paper into dry grass. That ignited the yard and once that was fully involved, it set fire to the house, which proceeded to burn to the ground. At least they got the toilet paper off the property. No one was injured, but it must have been quite the interesting phone call to the insurance company.

Bank Heist Goes Sour

Don't believe everything you read on the Internet.

One man was under the mistaken belief that rubbing lemon juice on his face would prevent it from being picked up by security cameras, so he juiced up and confidently proceeded to rob two banks before they caught him.

All they had to do was to be on the lookout for a guy with an extreme pucker.

Wichita Wash Out

Okay, you want to rob someone and you're not a politician, lawyer, or banker. So what do you do?

In the thievery business, target selection is very important. Banks have armed guards, cameras and snotty loan officers. Stores often have security personnel and surveillance systems and little old ladies on the street don't carry much cash, plus they can swing a mean hand bag. What to do? A laundromat- that's it!

That's what one young man figured when he strode into a Fabric Care Center and handed the lone employee a note, "This is a robbery!"

The clerk was unimpressed and warned the would-be holdup man that he had a gun. Disgusted, the crook stormed out of the store leaving the note on the counter.

In 10 minutes he was back, informing the clerk that now he too had a gun. The clerk went about his business as they argued a bit but at last, mortified, the man left.

About 10 minutes later, the man returned and defiantly poured himself a cup of coffee, snatched the holdup note from the counter and left, never to be seen again.

Maybe This is How Mrs. O'Leary's Cow REALLY Started the Chicago Fire

If you are a person of delicate sensibilities, you may wish to skip this item and go onto the next one. If not, hold on to your seat.

AP reported that a Dutch veterinarian was fined the equivalent of $240 for burning down a farm.

The conflagration began after the vet tried to convince the farmer that his cow was experiencing excessive flatulence. Wishing to make his point convincingly and having a bit of the showman in him, the vet lit the vented bodily methane. The startled cow became a "four-legged flame thrower" and ran wild, setting bales of hay aflame which caused the barn and then other buildings to go up in smoke resulting in $80,000 in damages.

The cow was reportedly unharmed but the farmer was pretty burned up over the whole experience.

> Chuck, stand up, let the people see you.
>
> -Joe Biden, to a man in a wheelchair

Things Don't Necessarily Go Better with Coke

A Pontiac, Michigan, drug defendant named Johns argued that he had been searched without a warrant.

The arresting office contended that the large bulge in the defendant's jacket could have been a gun and therefore gave him the right to search.

Johns protested that the statement was ridiculous and since he happened to be wearing the same jacket to court that day, he removed it and asked the judge to inspect it.

Sure enough, in the same pocket that the cop had spotted the bulge, the judge discovered a big bag of cocaine.

Justice was delayed temporarily while the judge, laughing so hard that he was in tears, adjourned the trial for five minutes so that he might compose himself.

So, where's the Cannes Film Festival being held this year?

-Christina Aguilera

Fast Food Chain Gets Itself Into a Pickle

Burger King tried an April fool's prank but managed only to put a Whoopee Cushion on the King's throne.

In 1998, they took a full page ad in *USA Today* introducing the left-handed Whopper.

Supposedly, all the condiments were rotated 180° to give their millions of southpaw customers the same burger experience everyone else had been enjoying for years.

It worked beyond the company's wildest dreams-taking it in fact all the way to a nightmare.

The restaurants suffered backed up lines and severe congestion with southpaw customers inquiring about the left-handed Whoppers and right-handed patrons returning to the counter to confirm if the orientation of their sandwiches was indeed correct.

Through all the delays and confusion, it never seemed to occur to anyone that the burger was round and therefore the same left-handed, right-handed or even upside-down.

Whale of a Tale

One of the inspirations for author Herman Melville's classic *Moby-Dick* was the true-life sinking of the whaling ship "Essex" by a whale in 1820. Captain George Pollard and several others aboard the ship resorted to cannibalism to survive the long ordeal.

Long after the tragedy, Pollard was approached by a relative of one of the lost crew members, who timidly asked whether the captain remembered him.

"Remember him!?" exclaimed Pollard. "Hell, I ate him!"

Tree Trouble

It was just after the holidays in Westfield, Massachusetts, when a woman called the police to say that her neighbors were having an extremely boisterous argument. The police officer at the scene reported that it was a neighbor who was alone and completely sober, but was having a major disagreement with his Christmas tree, which was giving him a tough time as he was taking it down.

What Do You Expect From Working For an Airline- A Golden Parachute?

Some corporations are all heart.

Facing bankruptcy, Northwest Airlines laid off thousands of workers but not before providing a sweet severance package consisting of a pamphlet suggesting ways for them to stretch their budgets.

"101 Ways To Save Money" was replete with such gems as when dumpster diving, "Don't be shy about pulling something you like out of the trash." Other tips included shredding old newspapers to make your own cat litter and inviting dates out for a walk in the woods as a low cost alternative to restaurants and movies.

With thinking like that, it's baffling to understand how the executives at a company that provided for people's comfort ever got themselves into bankruptcy in the first place.

I'm not anorexic. I'm from Texas.
Are there people from Texas who are anorexic?
I've never heard of one. And that includes me.

-Jessica Simpson

Hilarious Headlines

"Man Killed To Death" -*WBTV news*

•

"Council Calls in Counselors To Council Council Councillors" -*The Argus*

•

"One Armed Man Applauds The Kindness Of Strangers" -*Tulsa World*

•

"County To Pay $250,000 To Advertise Lack Of Funds" -*Register-Guard*

•

"Forecasters Call For Weather On Monday" -*Pittsburgh Post-Gazette*

•

"Hispanics Ace Spanish Tests" -*The Examiner*

•

"Bugs Flying Around With Wings Are Flying Bugs" -*Redwood County Extension Educator*

•

"Porn Star Sues Over Rear-End Collision" -*AP*

•

"Crack Found In Man's Buttocks" -*AP*

Rarely is the question asked,
"Is our children learning?"

-George W. Bush

"Illiteracy An Obstable, Study Finds"
-Washington Post

•

"Marijuana Issue Sent To Joint Committee"
-Toronto Star

•

"Homicide Victims Rarely Talk To Police"
-Express Times

•

"Local Man Fails Breathalyzer Test Despite
Eating Underwear" *-USA Today*

•

"Statistics Show Teen Pregnancy Drops Off
Significantly After Age 25" *-New York Post*

•

"Lady Gaga Fan Dies at Concert, Recovers"
-The Tennessean

•

"City Unsure Why the Sewer Smells"
-The Herald-Palladium (St. Joseph, Michigan)

•

"Alton Attorney Accidentally Sues Himself"
-Madison Record

•

"Poverty Meeting Attracts Poor Turnout"
-Gooding County Leader

•

"World Cup Shocker - USA Wins 1-1"
-New York Post

Bathroom Blooper

Foul Territory

What's worse than having your gold tooth fall into a toilet at Citi Field during a Mets game? Going in after it and having your arm stuck for hours as the high vacuum system continuously tries to flush you. A female Mets fan got into just that predicament, doing about as well in the john as the Mets were on the field. The plumber who installed the system had to be located and he finally managed to extract her after several hours of being flushed up to her armpit. She lost her tooth and the Mets lost the game- so ends the story in Flushing, New York.

Throwing This Up for Grabs

Biologically Appropriate Raw Food which trades under the name of BARF might be too much for you to swallow, but it doesn't bother pets at all.

BARF World pet foods produces a natural, healthy diet for dogs but they're seemingly horribly backwards when it comes to acronyms.

Then again, maybe they're crazy like a fox.

It's almost worth buying it just to brag to your friends that the only thing your dogs will eat is BARF.

Not Coming Through
in the Clutch

Delivery drivers make easy prey. After all, they're usually loaded with Chinese food or pizzas and those oh-so-lucrative tips.

But because of the ever-present risk that they might be armed with hot sauce, this particular trio of Massachusetts thieves decided to play it safe and go three on one.

Robbing the victim, they took off with both the take-out and the driver's keys.

Upon reaching the no doubt luxurious and lightning fast delivery car, they jumped in, planning to speed away into the night.

Except, according to *The Springfield Republican*, the car had a manual transmission and none of them knew how to drive it.

Their master plan never allowed for a stick shift in their stick up so they were just plain stuck.

> Movies are a fad. Audiences really
> want to see live actors on a stage.
>
> -Charlie Chaplin

True Tales of Clueless Crooks

Alexander Smith entered an Augusta, GA, bank and tried to open an account with a $1 million bill. Too bad there's no such thing as a $1 million bill.

• •

A thief who pilfered a valuable lamp from St. Patrick's Catholic Church in Winson Green, England, was caught on the surveillance video making the sign of the cross just before stealing the object.

• •

A Hicksville, NY, man was charged with petty larceny after a pet shop saleswoman heard chirping coming from his pants. When police arrived they discovered a pair of lovebirds in the man's pants. The suspect was promptly put behind bars. So were the lovebirds.

• •

In Georgia, a forty-one year-old man held up a gas station with his face partially covered. That might have worked with someone else, but the attendant on duty at the time was his daughter.

I'm not good with time. Like, if I ask you the time
and you say 'A quarter to 2' I wouldn't know.
Why can't you just say 2:30?

-Snooki

They say a criminal always returns to the scene of the crime, but not usually for this reason. A burglar had gotten away scot-free with the TV. The mistake he made that led to his arrest was coming back a few hours later to steal the remote.

• •

A New Jersey high school student felt that a snowstorm would be a good time to rob his local 7-11. He came up to the clerk, pulled a gun and made off with $50. He didn't get a chance to spend it though- the police merely followed his footprints from the store all the way to his front door.

• •

You've always heard that it takes money to make money. That apparently was true for a couple of New York bank robbers who couldn't afford decent transportation. Their junk heap getaway car had a "For Sale" notice in the window with their phone number written in large white letters which could be easily seen by one and all as they drove away. Hope they managed to unload the wreck because they won't be needing a car for the next five to ten years.

• •

Portsmouth, Rhode Island, police figured they had the right guy when they arrested a man for a string of vending machine robberies. By the time he posted his $400 bond they felt even more confident. It was completely in coins.

This Time the Judge Will Throw the Boot At Him

1999: The world cowered in fear of the Y2K bug, the Clinton-Lewinsky brouhaha reached its peak and the Stride Rite shoe store in Toms River, NJ, was robbed by a man named Miller.

Flash ahead 15 years: The world cowers in fear of the bed bug, Clinton and Lewinsky haven't brewed any haha in years and the Stride Rite shoe store in Toms River, NJ, was robbed by a man named Miller- the very same Miller who robbed it a decade and a half before.

Seems Miller spent 15 years in the big house for the previous robbery and having served his time, was released.

Immediately he caught a bus, returned to the shoe store and robbed it again, making off with $389.

Again he was captured in almost no time at all and the police recovered the booty.

You'd think after 15 years, he'd have come up with a better plan.

Yogi Must Really Miss Boo Boo

A Minnesota man complained to the police that he had been molested- by a bear!

The victim was hiking through the Kabetogama State Forest when he encountered a black bear. According to the official report, the man remembered to drop to the ground and play dead.

The bear must have found this action particularly alluring because it immediately grabbed him by his sweater collar and dragged him back to its cave where the bear proceeded to, shall we say, "Have a few Kodiak Moments" with the terrified hiker, teaching him where cubs come from.

After a little while, the man reported, the bear went out for food - or a smoke- and he escaped his "grizzly" encounter.

He phoned the police to report his abduction but slowly realized as the call went on that he couldn't file charges against a bear anyway and simply hung up.

Try to use a little tact, you fathead.

-Burt Reynolds

How You Gonna Keep Them Down on the Farm?

Generally farming is a demanding but relatively safe profession. The carrots rarely fight back. Not every farmer leads a peaceful life though. It depends what you're farming.

In South Africa, a reptile farm got more than it bargained for when a flood released 15,000 of its "crops."

The problem was that the "crops" were crocs and 15,000 crocodiles is a lot of teeth and snapping jaws to turn loose on your neighbors.

About half were eventually recaptured but the other 7,500 are making South Africans think twice about dipping their tootsies in the Limpopo River.

Why call him Joe? Every Tom, Dick, and Harry is called Joe.

-Samuel Goldwyn

Bathroom Blooper

Bus Flush

Though buses are an efficient way to move a lot of people, they're not always the thing you want in front of you in heavy traffic. With their loud diesel engines, belching fumes, brakes squealing, and the total blockage of any air or visibility, creeping along behind them can be unpleasant. But one Ohio family suffered far more than most for sharing a roadway with a bus. A Greyhound bus they had been following suddenly discharged the contents of its toilets into the open sunroof of their SUV. At last word, their lawyer was seeking $300,000 in damages but the case may never come to court; the family's not out of the shower yet.

Korea No Fan of Fans

The Korea Consumer Protection Board issued a consumer safety alert regarding sleeping in closed rooms with an electric fan. In Korea, even medical authorities believe that fans can be lethal, causing death by suffocation or hypothermia. Most of the danger is believed to be to those using a fan in a closed bedroom. Koreans think of it as kind of a five-bladed Boogeyman.

Rest easy Korea. Fortunately, a fan surrounded by an air conditioner is considered completely safe.

Putting Lipstick on a Pig

Flagler County, Florida, has beautiful beaches, swaying palms and lots of wild pigs (even when it's not Spring Break). It also is loaded with hunters determined to bring home the bacon.

The story of one such hunter gained widespread notoriety in 2012. He was tracking a wounded pig while his girlfriend was picking wild oranges. Thinking he had his quarry in his sights, he fired. Turns out he had mistaken his girlfriend for the boar and shot her in the leg instead.

Fortunately, the hunter's girlfriend was a cardiac nurse and knew immediately what first aid she needed for her very serious wound. Unfortunately for the couple, the horror of the accident became a nightmare of national attention.

The Tonight Show's Jay Leno said, "I don't know what is worse for the girl: having your boyfriend shoot you in the legs or saying the reason he did it was that he mistook you for a hog."

The hunter's girlfriend forgave him in a love-conquers-all ending. But the embarrassing attention didn't fade until another Florida man committed an atrocity that galvanized the public interest– the story of the naked man who tried to eat a homeless man's face.

Weird Weed News

The *Pittsburgh Post-Gazette* reported that police were called by a 21-year-old man who suspected that he'd just been duped. He told the cops that the marijuana he bought from a street dealer tasted "nasty," and he wanted the police to confirm that the pot was not fake. Fortunately for him, it was.

Branch Robbed by Tree

A bank robber in Manchester, New Hampshire, thought dressing up as a tree was the perfect disguise. He duct-taped branches to his head and body and leaves to his face, then went in for the stick up. Fortunately, the security camera didn't have the old problem of not being able to see the forest for the trees and got enough shots of his face for police to root him out. Whether he was a shady character or a tree-time loser, he took the fall and they probably won't spring him for a long, long time.

I was asked to come to Chicago because Chicago is one of our 52 states.

-Raquel Welch

Squidlock

This is one giant octopus that got lots of ink.

Fans of the 1950s giant mutant monster creature feature films may remember a scene in *Gorgo* where the captured creature is trucked through the streets of London on its way to be displayed at Piccadilly Circus. The resulting sensation turned central London into a mob scene.

Recently, life imitated art when a large truck carrying a giant octopus broke down in the middle of a busy intersection at rush hour, snarling traffic and sparking off a storm of speculation on the news and social media.

The giant octopus was a model of course but the monstrous traffic jam it caused was real enough to elicit an apology from Betfair, the gambling web site which was in the process of moving the huge octopod for a publicity stunt.

Considering the crowds and the coverage, it seems to have worked better than expected.

I believe that people would be
alive today if there were a death penalty.

-Nancy Reagan

McMad

A Toledo, Ohio, woman went to a McDonald's drive-through at 6 a.m. and wanted an order of McNuggets. The woman became enraged when told it was too early so she tried to punch the attendant, then punched another employee and finally hurled a bottle through the drive-through window. Instead of getting her McNuggets, she got 60 days.

From the Classifieds

• Wanted: Human cannonball – must be able to travel

• Amana washer $100. Owned by clean bachelor who seldom washed.

• WAITRESS NEEDED. Must be 18 years old with 20 years experience.

• USED TOMBSTONE, perfect for someone named Homer HendelBergenHeinzel. One only.

• Tired of working for only $9.75 per hour? We offer profit-sharing and flexible hours. Starting pay, $7-9 per hour.

• HAVE VIAGRA. Need woman. Any woman between 18 & 80.

• Chronically Overweight? 6 p.m., 522 N. Eighth St., Sheboygan...Bring your own chair.

Phoney Business

A United Kingdom based mobile phone insurance
company shared a list of its most amusing
lost and damaged phone claims.

An undertaker from London reported his phone
as lost, but called the next day to say never mind.
He found it inside a coffin, next to a body that
was due to be buried shortly afterwards.

•

A builder said he lost his phone, but later called
to withdraw the claim after a customer of his said
they'd heard a phone ringing inside the wall of
their new extension. He'd left it inside the wall
cavity and the customer was kind enough to let
him remove the phone and patch the wall up.

•

A farmer in Devon claimed his phone had
disappeared inside the back end of his cow while
he was using the flashlight app in assisting the
birth of a calf. The phone reappeared, but was
damaged.

•

A woman from Nottingham reported that she
accidentally baked her Nokia 6303i into her
daughter's birthday cake.

•

A Bristol woman claimed that her Blackberry's
"vibration" mode broke while she was using it as
an adult toy.

A construction worker said his iPhone fell out of his back pocket when he pulled his jeans down before sitting on the toilet. Unaware, he flushed the toilet with the phone in it. The phone didn't go down the tubes, but it did have some serious water damage.

•

A man claimed he'd been filming monkeys from his car window in a safari park with his HTC One X when one of them climbed on the roof and snatched it.

•

A couple lost their phone over the side of a cruise ship while attempting to take a selfie as they re-enacted the "I'm the King of the World!" scene from the movie *Titanic*.

•

A woman from Birmingham informed mobileinsurance.co.uk that the lost phone she'd earlier reported had actually turned up in her fridge, next to the milk on the middle shelf.

A zebra does not change its spots.

-Al Gore, attacking President Bush, 1992

AT&T with the Queen

Oh, to be invited to tea with the Queen of England. It is the dream of any loyal subject.

As you might imagine, certain protocols must be observed. For example, remembering to turn off your phone.

One invitee recently was reminded of that courtesy in the most embarrassing way possible.

As the ceremony progressed, the phone began ringing and the Queen abruptly halted the proceedings with a withering, "You may want to get that. It could be someone important."

Eternal Embarrassment

Cops raided an English pub looking for a drug dealer. The bobbies thought they found the culprit and pounced on an elderly man with a bag of white powder, only to find out that the substance was actually the ashes of his late wife, Alice, which he carried everywhere.

TV won't last because people will soon get tired of staring at a plywood box every night.

-Darryl Zanuck, 20th Century Fox
movie studio head, 1946

Why Not Use a Shotgun? There's Less Chance of Missing the Can

The degree of someone's good judgment seems to be inversely proportional to that person's good luck. If that were not true, the man in the following item wouldn't be alive.

Initiations can be demeaning, embarrassing or just plain stupid. Pinning the meter in the red zone of the latter category was the right of passage required to join an Oregon organization named Mountain Men Anonymous.

Apparently, as part of the induction ceremony, a young fellow named Roberts agreed to let a friend shoot a beer can off his head. Of course the can was empty. All the beer cans in the area were empty, if you get the drift.

As you might imagine, the arrow missed its mark, instead piercing Robert's eye and continuing on through his brain, which apparently was an uninvolved bystander at the time. With the arrow through his head, Roberts resembled an early Steve Martin comedy bit.

Taken to Portland's University Hospital and placed in the hands of gifted surgeons, Roberts survived. In his case, the arrow in his brain didn't constitute an injury to a vital organ.

Bathroom Blooper

The Governor Can't Pardon You From the Sentence Handed Down by Fate

Sometimes blunders are just plain bad luck. Consider the case of Michael Godwin, who served many years on South Carolina's death row due to a murder conviction. He was soon to be sent to the electric chair when word came that his sentence was commuted to life in prison. Having a new lease on life, he enjoyed the small things once again- the fresh air of the prison yard, carving a gun from a bar of soap and watching the small TV set the prison allowed him in his cell. One day, while sitting on the cell's metal toilet, he was trying to get the TV to work when he accidentally bit into a wire and was electrocuted. In many ways, an electric toilet would be a less controversial method of capital punishment than an electric chair. Everyone agrees that when ya gotta go, ya gotta go.

Driving While Distracted

According to the *Winfield Register*, an Illinois newspaper, Stanley R. Zegel was stopped at a red light when he was rear-ended by another car. The offending driver maintained that he was on his way to attend a nearby court-ordered driving-improvement course and got sidetracked while looking at a paper for its street address.

Ball Point Ball Up

Parker Pen debuted in Mexico with high hopes. They introduced themselves with their tagline: "It won't leak in your pocket and embarrass you."

So far, so good but it needed to be translated into Spanish. That's when the trouble started.

The result was thousands of ads proclaiming in Spanish, "It won't leak in your pocket and make you pregnant."

As far as Parker Pens in Mexico went, that's all she wrote.

A Bite Out of History

In 1877, President U.S. Grant took a world cruise so that he could meet and greet with people from all over the planet. Unfortunately, not too much meeting and greeting went on. During the excursion, Grant's false teeth fell overboard, leaving him with little bark and no bite.

Although it is...an interesting novelty, the telephone has no commercial application.

-J.P. Morgan, to Alexander Graham Bell

Party Popper

If there were an Olympics for stupidity, no one else would even bother showing up.

This was out there even for someone who was not only a moronic jerk but also roaring drunk.

As the Kincaid, West Virginia, evening wore on and the party got wilder, out came the blasting caps.

Never a good sign.

While one partier at the soiree was attempting to set off a blasting cap in an aquarium using a battery, our Gold Mental winner declared that he'd demonstrate the proper way to detonate the explosive. With that, he popped it in his mouth and bit down.

Miraculously he survived- but only just barely. He probably won't be attending any more wild parties as this one turned out to be a real blast.

Predictions are difficult, especially about the future.

-Yogi Berra

Disoriented Express

Africa can be hot, dry and dusty. So you might understand a driver navigating the back roads of the Dark Continent seeking some refreshment along the way.

Of course it wasn't wise for the Zimbabwean bus driver to choose hard liquor as his beverage but that was only the start of his trouble.

He was drinking and driving while transporting a busload of mental patients to a new facility. The patients might have had mental issues but they weren't stupid. While the driver was out imbibing, they had made themselves scarce.

When he returned from his extended stopover, he discovered his bus was empty. Of course the driver did what any well-trained Zimbabwean bus driver would do in a similar situation. He offered free rides to anyone and everyone until he had refilled his bus with townsfolk excited by the novelty of a bus ride.

He continued on to his destination, informing the doctors that this particular group of "patients" suffered from bizarre fantasies and would probably deny that they belonged in a hospital.

It took three days to discover the ruse.

Oval Office Oopsies

"I'll be long gone before some smart person ever figures out what happened inside this Oval Office." -President George W. Bush

"The world is more like it is now then it ever has before." -President Dwight Eisenhower

"You know the one thing that's wrong with this country? Everyone gets a chance to have their fair say." -President Bill Clinton

"Well, I learned a lot....I went down to (Latin America) to find out from them and (learn) their views. You'd be surprised. They're all individual countries." -President Ronald Reagan

"I've now been in 57 states -- I think one left to go." -President Barack Obama (on the campaign trail)

"Being president is like running a cemetery: you've got a lot of people under you and nobody's listening." -President Bill Clinton

"When more and more people are thrown out of work, unemployment results." -President Calvin Coolidge

"They misunderestimated me."
-President George W. Bush

They Thought "Freedom of the Press" Meant Freedom to Press on Duct Tape

It's not the first time a sticky situation has been handled with duct tape.

Officials at a Tucson high school were shocked and appalled when they got the expensive yearbooks back from the printers and only then discovered the blunt comments made by many of the graduating class who'd be moving on and had little to lose.

Not being able to find any white-out, they did the only thing they could and turned to the handyman's helper for a last-minute bit of censorship.

Hastily torn crude strips of tape covered the offending passages. In this case, you might refer to the duct tape as the dis-honor roll.

Of all the things I've lost,
it's my mind I miss the most.

-Ozzy Osbourne

The Old Skin Game

Many try to hide their crime but this guy's crime was hide.

A 54-year-old Pennsylvania skin-graft salesman was suspected of stealing $350,000 of skin from Mercy hospital in Philadelphia. To put it in perspective, that's almost enough to rebuild the old Al Roker and the classic Chris Christie.

In a crime that bordered on graft, the salesman reportedly got the cops' dander up once they sweated the facts out of him. Someone's in for a bruising cross examination and however it goes, it'll probably be a close shave. Everyone's got skin in the game but no one wants a rash judgment. They've barely scratched the surface and you never know when a new wrinkle might turn up.

The accused said that it was no skin off his nose but that's a pore excuse.

The United States has much
to offer the third world war.

-Ronald Reagan (He meant "Third World.")

Bathroom Blooper

Getting Caught With His Pants Down

Drinking and dumbness don't mix and together they really shouldn't be combined with crime. A British burglar discovered that when he tried some second story work while sloshed. He'd already led police on an extended high speed chase around Sunderland when he decided to top off his evening by breaking into a home and picking up some swag to cover the gas money. But he was sleepy and as they say, great goings-in have great comings-out so he plopped down on the toilet. Police, spotting the broken window in their search area, entered the home and found the suspect dozing, still atop the porcelain perch with his pants around his ankles.

Racist Recipe

A major Australian publisher spent a fortune recalling and reprinting a popular cookbook with one tiny but absolutely horrific misprint. When making one of the pasta dishes, it directed readers to "add salt and freshly ground black people."

Apparently autocorrect is not also politically correct.

Insurance Insanity

The following are actual insurance company claims.

"Going to work at 7 a.m. this morning I drove out of my drive straight into a bus. The bus was five minutes early."

•

"The car in front hit the pedestrian but he got up so I hit him again."

•

"I pulled away from the side of the road, glanced at my mother-in-law and headed over the embankment."

•

"I collided with a stationary truck coming the other way."

•

"In an attempt to kill a fly, I drove into a telephone pole."

•

"An invisible car came out of nowhere, struck my car and vanished."

•

"I thought my window was down, but I found it was up when I put my head through it."

•

"As I approached an intersection a sign suddenly appeared in a place where no stop sign had ever appeared before."

"I told the police I wasn't injured, but on removing my hat found that I had a fractured skull."

•

"I was sure the old fellow would never make it to the other side of the road when I struck him."

•

"The pedestrian had no idea which way to run as I ran over him."

•

"I saw a slow moving, sad faced old gentleman as he bounced off the roof of my car."

•

"The gentleman behind me struck me on the backside. He then went to rest in a bush with just his rear end showing."

•

"The pedestrian ran for the pavement, but I got him."

•

"The accident was caused by me waving to the man I hit last week."

•

"I knocked over a man; he admitted it was his fault for he had been knocked down before."

Solutions are not the answer.

-Richard Nixon

Jersey Couple Goes
Out With a Bang

You're in New Jersey, it's the wee hours of the morning and you don't feel like going to a diner. What else is there to do?

Bored by just driving around at 2 a.m., a Garden State couple decided to liven things up a bit with a quarter stick of dynamite they just happened to have on them (don't ask- this IS New Jersey we're talking about).

The plan was simple:

1) Light it.
2) Throw it out the window.
3) See what happens.

It was the second part that gave them the most trouble. In retrospect, perhaps they should have started the plan with "Open window."

Where do you go in Jersey in the middle of the night? Try the hospital.

I tell you flatly, he can't last.

-Jackie Gleason, of Elvis Presley

All the News That's Fit to Misprint

Apologies from some of your favorite newspapers

"An article about Ivana Trump and her spending habits misstated the number of bras she buys. It is two dozen black, two dozen beige, and two dozen white, not two thousand of each."
-The New York Times

"A May 31 Metro article abut the Scripps National Spelling Bee misspelled last year's winning word. The correct spelling is serrefine."
-Washington Post

"There was a typo in lawyer Ed Morrison's ad. His logo is: 'Your case is no stronger than your attorney,' not 'stranger.'"
-Tulsa (Oklahoma) *Gusher*

"*The Ottawa Citizen* and *Southam News* wish to apologize for our apology to Mark Steyn, published Oct. 22. In correcting the incorrect statements about Mr. Steyn published Oct. 15, we incorrectly published the incorrect correction. We accept and regret that our original regrets were unacceptable and we apologize to Mr. Steyn."

Bathroom Blooper

Smart Throne

Maybe someone who pays $6,000 for a toilet has it coming. The Satis toilet must give a lot of "Satis-faction" if its price tag is anything to go by. The luxury throne comes with piped in music, automatic flushing, bidet spray and a choice of fragrances. It is also controlled by a wireless Android app called "My Satis." Therein squats the toad. Anyone with the app and Bluetooth can hijack your john. A merry prankster might simply keep flushing the opulent pot, running up the water bill or get more creative with the johnny japes by opening and closing the seat at inopportune times or unexpectedly switching on the bidet or air-dry functions. Look at it as the high-tech update to the old Saran Wrap over the toilet bowl gag.

Another From the Florida Files

Some days things go well and others, you just can't get arrested- well, you can but a lot of other bad stuff happens first.

Such was the case with a bank robber named Jones who walked into a Miami bank, pulled a gun and demanded money.

The teller complied and Jones was soon out the bank door and embarking on the getaway phase of his adventure. That's where things started to go wrong.

First, mimicking every bad crime movie ever, he stuffed the gun down his pants, never thinking that it would go off. But it did.

As if that wasn't enough to rattle him, the distracted Jones stepped into the street where he was immediately struck by a delivery van knocking out his gold teeth. He managed to drag himself away, but the escape was to no avail as he left enough DNA at the crime scene to start his own Jurassic Park of stupid criminals.

It wasn't long before the FBI caught up to him and the hat, gun, blood and teeth left at the crime scene, were submitted into evidence.

The greatest indignity of the whole sad affair was that, according to Reuters, the FBI added insult to injury by nicknaming him, "The Bumbling Bank Robber."

Everything that can be invented
has been invented.

-Charles H. Duell, Commissioner of
U.S. Office of Patents, 1899

Ball Park Prank Puts
Buns in a Sling

The Phillie Phanatic got into hot water again.

Baseball's most-sued mascot filmed a commercial at Philadelphia's Citizens Bank Park just before a Phillies game against the Atlanta Braves. The stunt involved firing heavily wrapped hot dogs from a launcher. Somehow, three of the duct tape encased franks of unknown origin wound up outside the park, appearing suspicious enough for police to clear the stadium and call in the bomb squad.

It was only after the hot dogs were given the works in a controlled detonation that they were identified as such. Apparently, they plump when you explode 'em.

The spokesman for the Phillies management said that although they didn't relish the decision, it was better to be safe than sorry so everyone would come out a wiener.

I don't want to run the risk of ruining what is a lovely recession.

-George H.W. Bush in a 1992 campaign speech in New Jersey (He meant to say "reception.")

Game Show Goofs

On *Wheel of Fortune*, all of the letters but one were shown in the following puzzle:

'_T TAKES ONE TO KNOW ONE.'

The contestant said, "I'd like to solve the puzzle."

Host Pat Sajak replied, "This shouldn't be too hard. Go ahead."

The contestant said: "E.T. takes one to know one."

• •

'Tool Time' was the category on *Jeopardy!* when its host, Alex Trebek, read this 'answer': "This term for a long-handled gardening tool can also mean an immoral pleasure seeker."

The show's most famous contestant, Ken Jennings, followed up with this: "What's a ho?" (The correct answer, or question, was "rake.")

• •

Steve Harvey, on *Family Feud*: "Name something that follows the word 'pork.'"

Contestant: "Cupine"

Harvey: "Pork...Cupine- This is the greatest answer I've ever heard!"

Slippery Character

A New Zealand man got stuck in the grease vent of a fish and chips shop in Papanui. It was either a burglary attempt or a guy with one serious 2 a.m. attack of the munchies.

The grease extractor vent running from just above the deep fat fryers in the kitchen up to the roof seemed the perfect way to get into the shop. The man climbed in, realizing only too late that the chimney's interior was completely coated with about an inch of grease. He instantly plummeted down to the fan where one of the support struts lodged in his, shall we say, lower bifurcation, its way greatly eased by the extremely slippery conditions.

Trapped in the cramped vent, his foot dangling just inches over the fryer oil and an unwelcome addition to his anatomy, the pomaded perpetrator spent a few hours trying to extricate himself but to no avail.

When his cries for help were finally heard, the fire department responded, spending several more hours tearing the slimy vent apart to release him. Thoroughly coated with the same grease, their uniforms and gear had to be sent off for special cleaning.

As far as the oily burglar goes, he was taken to the police station where officers declined to grill him fearing a grease fire.

A Slow Day at the Office

Things were quiet, things were peaceful. Everything had been set up and there wasn't much to do.

German General Rommel, famed as "The Desert Fox," decided to take the opportunity to return home for his wife's June birthday and leave the coastal defenses to his subordinates.

The Third Reich's greatest general knew that his wife would be thrilled to see him home from defending Normandy and 1944 would be a year they would always remember.

He was right. That was one birthday they'd always remember. Seems the Allies even planned a little surprise party.

Always be sincere, even if you don't mean it.

-Harry S Truman

This Crime Took a Lot of Crust

You too can become a criminal in 30 minutes or less. Just do what these Tuscaloosa men did. Rob a pizza delivery guy and steal his money along with all his pizzas. They even got the bag that kept them warm.

Oh, by the way, when you carry out your own pizza heist, just don't do what these men from Tuscaloosa did: call for delivery from your own house.

Makes the Heart Go Honda

Over a million Honda owner's manuals carry a number to call The National Highway Traffic Administration. The number is wrong. Actually, it's worse than wrong. It connects the caller to a line promoting adult phone services.

So if you call and are greeted by that super sultry voice, just remember times are tough and Siri really needs that second job.

I never apologize.
I'm sorry, but that's just the way I am.

-Homer Simpson

Bathroom Blooper

Long Relief

While Jeff Liefer was a first round draft pick of the White Sox in 1995, his most memorable baseball moment came as a member of the minor league Indianapolis Indians. In 2004, the first basemen went to the bathroom in the clubhouse between innings. He couldn't get out. It wouldn't have been so bad if the Indians simply put in a replacement, but instead, the game was delayed 20 minutes until someone got Liefer out. Of the incident, he remarked, "I don't want to be remembered as the guy who got stuck in the bathroom." Sorry, Jeff.

The South Shall Rise Again- And You Might Too

The South is nothing if not polite. There's a certain Southern charm in everything they do.

Take for example this food stamp discontinuation notice sent from Greenville, South Carolina:

"Your food stamps will be stopped effective March 1992 because we received notice that you passed away. May God bless you. You may reapply if there is a change in your circumstances."

-Department of Social Services

Police Blotter Bloopers

For every supervillain, there are thousands of stuporvillains. Here's what the cops have to deal with between donuts...

A Willow Creek, Montana, woman was taken into custody for attacking her boyfriend because she didn't like what he said about her in his sleep. After beating him with a shotgun, she shot out his front tire and smashed his windshield. Talk about a rude awakening!

•

In Tallahassee, Florida, police discovered a nude man walking a dog. When asked what he was doing, he answered that Allah told him to exercise the pooch and watch a Bruce Willis movie. Not wishing the man to die hard, the cop simply tased him and sent him for a psych evaluation. The dog declined any comment.

•

Miami Beach police report a case in which a homeless man broke into a car and stole a credit card. He then went into a nearby bar and tried to use it to buy a beer. It might have worked if the card hadn't belonged to the bartender.

What's a guy to do when two dates show up at the same time? Call 911. That's what a Colorado Springs man did when his girlfriend, who came home unexpectedly, and someone he had found on craigslist were about to meet and spoil his handy little arrangement. Thinking quickly, he dialed the police and reported that the craigslist girl was a burglar. Neither police nor the woman from the online ad took kindly to his attempt to cover his booty call.

•

A 45 year old Morrow, Georgia, man dressed as an elf went to a local mall and threatened Santa with dynamite. Police report that he politely waited on line before reaching Santa with the threat. Santa immediately alerted mall security and the elf was led away. The suspect better double-check that the lump of coal in his stocking this Christmas isn't made of C-4.

I would like to spank director Spike Jonze.

-Meryl Streep, misreading a faxed acceptance speech at the British American Film and Television Awards

Hollywood Goes to War

The fog of war blew in from the ocean and settled over L.A. even though the conflict was thousands of miles away.

"Air Battle Over Los Angeles" screamed the headline in the *Los Angeles Examiner* in 1942.

The town was on edge from a naval intelligence estimate that an attack could come at any moment.

Hysteria ran rampant throughout the city at the supposedly imminent Japanese invasion. It turned out that our own airbursts were mistaken for enemy action in the frantic searchlights.

The populace panicked and much damage was done but at least Hollywood recovered some of the expense 40 years later as Steven Spielberg got an all-star comedy movie out of the incident - though the title, *1941*, was a year off.

Chemistry is a class you take in
high school or college, where you figure out
two plus two is ten, or something.

-Dennis Rodman

The Great Lame Robbery

A bungling Brit won a two-and-a-half year, all expenses paid staycation at the local ill-mannered house for making a snap decision to hold up a bank with a bread knife just after giving the teller his full name and address.

Those cash drawers at Barclay's bank looked too good to resist and the trip to the bank to change his address blossomed into a full-on bank robbery.

He didn't get away with anything but was successful in one regard- his address has now officially been changed for him.

No Sanity Clause

A California man tried to gain access to his ex-wife's house in a most unusual way. He used the chimney. Alas, he was no Santa and his bowl full of jelly got wedged most of the way down.

His ex-wife now had him where she wanted him. What to do? What to do? She could either stoke up the fireplace or call the police. Either way, he was going to get burned.

Fortunately, she chose the latter and her former hubby was pried out with minor injuries and severely bruised pride.

Govern-Mental

On June 8, 1959, a submarine quietly surfaced
in the warm waters off Florida and fired a guided
missile at the heart of the United States.
Unerringly, it streaked through the air and found
its target, delivering an unmistakable message to
President Eisenhower along with thousands of
pieces of mail.

It's bad enough when a post office employee goes
"postal," armed with a handful of packing peanuts
and a prepaid envelope capable of inflicting some
nasty paper cuts, but how about if they were
packing a guided missile?

That could have been our reality if the Rocket
Mail post office program had been continued.

In one of the screwiest ideas ever cooked up in
Washington, DC, the post office was armed with
a ballistic missile in the late '50s as a new weapon
in the struggle against slow mail service. Maybe
the Postmaster General took his title a bit too
literally.

The idea was to use the missile to transport a lot
of mail from one place to another really quickly,
sort of an ICBM update to the Pony Express. Talk
about pushing the outside of the envelope!

The test firing went off without a hitch and the feared Russian retaliation of launching more dogs into space to chase our mail rockets never materialized. Still, the impracticalities were obvious and the idea soon went down in flames.

But don't be too relieved. Someday soon, the doorbell may ring twice and you'll answer to a black NSA drone with a "special delivery" from the Dead Letter Office.

Forget the Burning Bush, We Got a Melting Menorah

What could be more respectful of one of the world's oldest religions than selling its followers Menorahs featuring zany M&M characters? How about one that unexpectedly bursts into flame?

Mars had to recall over a thousand of the M&M menorahs after some sparked, melted and set the Star of David ablaze.

Perhaps in this case M&M stood for Meshuga Mayhem.

> I don't think anyone should write
> his autobiography until after he is dead.
>
> -Samuel Goldwyn

Craps!

Harrah's casino in Joliet, Illinois, may be the exception to the gambler's rule that the house always wins.

While math strictly controls the odds on all the casino's games, giving the house the edge, it has no say over the companies that print the casino's coupons.

As a promotion, Harrah's planned to send coupons worth $15 or $20 to 11,000 of their loyal customers.

As it happened, the printer sent out 11,000 vouchers each for $525 in cash.

It was a safe bet that Harrah's would balk at honoring the coupons, but the Illinois Gaming Board ruled that they must accept them.

It turned out to be a monumentally bad deal for the casino, costing them about $6 million.

It's not that I dislike many people.
It's just that I don't like many people.

–Bryant Gumbel

We're Gonna Need a Bigger... Golf Cart?

Think your golf course has mean water hazards? Consider then the Carbrook Golf Club in Brisbane, Australia. Their course comes complete with man-eating sharks.

Some time ago, the course was flooded when a river broke its banks. When the waters receded, a number of bull sharks, one of the most dangerous and aggressive species on earth, were left behind. They now thrive at the course.

They proved such a novelty that the greens man tosses them raw meat presumably to reduce their appetite for raw golfers.

Not Having It His Way

According to the *Ann Arbor News*, a man walked into a local Burger King, flashed a gun and demanded money. The clerk told him that he couldn't open the register without a food order.

The flustered thief blurted out, "Onion rings." The clerk replied that onion rings weren't available for breakfast. The frustrated crook then turned and stormed out of the store.

Bathroom Blooper

Flush With Evidence

A Jensen Beach, Florida, police officer was searching a suspect's home when nature called. This was one of those calls that you just had to answer- even in the line of police duty. The cop used the suspect's bathroom but when he tried to flush, the toilet wouldn't cooperate. Taking the top off the tank, there was a gun and several clips of ammunition stuffed down inside. The crook was arrested and probably charged with interfering with police business.

Have the Construction Workers Heard About This?

Sometimes a law is loony not for its intent but for the impossibility of enforcing it. For instance, New York City's fine for flirting. It's not fine to flirt; it's a fine if you flirt- a $25 fine for the first offense.

Upon the second conviction of walking down the street and turning around to "look at a woman in that way," the prescribed punishment is mandatory horse blinders to be worn at all times while in public.

It could work. Blinders would be difficult to wedge a hard hat over.

Just Sue It

A man sued Nike for $100 million because they failed to include a warning label advising that the shoes could be used as a dangerous weapon.

The Portland, Oregon, man's occupation, in the nicest possible terms, involved the representation of women who were in the profession of providing companionship for various gentlemen. When one of the clients reneged on payment, the plaintiff instigated his normal financial recovery procedure by stomping on the client's face.

He professed to be shocked at the extent of the injuries and believed that Nike was negligent in failing to caution him that their shoes, when used with great force upside the head, may cause injury.

With any luck, Nike can get the case booted out of court.

Listen, everyone is entitled to my opinion.

-Madonna

Label Lunacy

Warning labels are carefully crafted by lawyers,
but from the consumer's perspective,
they are almost unbelievably dumb.
Here's a collection of some of the silliest:

Birthday card for a 1 year old:
Warning! Not suitable For Children Under 3 Due
To Small Parts

•

From a prescription bottle for a dog:
Use care when operating a car or dangerous
machinery

•

On a can of pepper spray: May irritate eye

•

Spotted on a Razor scooter:
Warning: This product moves when used

•

Seen at the YMCA:
Hair dryers are for hair on the head only

•

On a Shrek shirt transfer:
Do not iron while wearing shirt

I should have read it before it came out.

-Charles Barkley, on being misquoted
in his autobiography

From a thermometer package:
Once used rectally, the thermometer should not be used orally

•

Warning on an automobile sunshield:
Do not drive with sunshield in place

•

On Play for Fun Brand Flying Ring:
Do not launch or throw in the direction of other people

•

On a curling iron: For external use only

•

U.S. Consumer Product Safety Commission directive on how to use laptop computers:
Do not use your computer on your lap

•

From a Jet Ski owner's manual:
Never use a lit match or open flame to check fuel level

•

On a 500-piece jigsaw puzzle:
Some assembly required

•

On rat poison label:
Warning: has been found to cause cancer in laboratory mice

Groupon Gets Clipped

When Google offers you $6 billion for your new business maybe you should take it.

That's what Groupon founder Andrew Mason found out after he declined Google's offer and then watched business conditions and operational problems reduce the value of the company by nearly 40%.

Mason took the company public and although he struggled mightily with Groupon's issues, he never redeemed himself with stockholders and was eventually fired.

Tattoo a Dead Giveaway

The police in Billings, Montana, were looking for a murder suspect named Sterling F. Wolfname. When they found someone at a shelter who matched his description, they asked the man if he was Wolfname. The man assured them he wasn't, but the cops concluded that the guy wasn't coming clean when they saw this tattoo plastered on his head: Wolfname.

DUI-I-I-I

Readington Township, NJ, police conducted a routine traffic stop late one night, smelled alcohol and arrested the driver.

At the jail, the woman called her friend to bail her out. When her friend arrived, police suspected that she too had been drinking. She was tested and arrested as well.

When it came time for her call, she phoned another friend who, you guessed it, was inebriated as well. The bars he was put behind obviously weren't the first he'd seen that evening.

After much calling, they finally found someone they knew who was both willing to come down to get them in the middle of the night and who also had not been drinking.

Could this be the way to finally get drunk drivers off the road? Just catch one and have them call all their buddies down to the police station.

> The president has kept all of the promises he intended to keep.
>
> -George Stephanopolous

Getting Stuck with the Quill

No good deed goes unpunished. A Brazilian man's pregnant wife was afraid of entering her home because an opossum was blocking the entrance.

Being a gallant and gentle soul, the Rio de Janeiro man took a light swipe at the creature to shoo him from the doorway.

That's when he found out that neither he nor his wife were very good at animal recognition.

When he yanked back his hand in agony, he discovered that the "opossum" was actually a porcupine- a porcupine that was missing 400 quills because they were now embedded in the man's hand.

At the hospital, he had the quills removed and received three shots of anesthetic but without much effect on the intense pain.

Next time you can be sure he'll use a broom.

> I have opinions of my own -strong opinions-
> but I don't always agree with them.
>
> -George W. Bush

Bathroom Blooper

Just Dropping In

A woman in Russia was relaxing in her tub and had just dozed off when the apparently rotten timbers under her apartment floor suddenly gave way and the tub fell into the living room of the rather surprised couple below. The woman sustained only a minor injury. Perhaps her bubble bath acted as lots of tiny little airbags.

You've Got Fail

When AOL acquired Time-Warner in 2000, it was the biggest corporate merger in history. It combined the pre-eminent corporation of the Internet and a multifaceted media giant into a juggernaut of movies, print, music and online synergies worth $300 billion.

Management's goal was to maximize the leverage afforded by both the production and worldwide distribution of content.

By 2009, the company was worth less than $40 billion, a $260 billion loss for a decade's work.

All because the cable guy couldn't peg the installation time any closer than somewhere between 9 a.m. and 5 p.m.

Off Key

When you are given the key to the city, it is the ultimate expression of respect. It is a warm, welcoming gesture of affection by the city's populace and their elected representatives.

Back in 1980, Detroit gave a momentous Motown honor to a man whose principles always lived up to the loftiest ethical standards of many auto dealers and car salespersons around the country. That man was Saddam Hussein.

Bullet Boo Boo

The only thing that stops a bad insect with many legs is a good guy with many arms.

That must have been what was going through an Oklahoma man's mind when he drew his rifle on a millipede. That's right, one of those little bugs.

The overkill backfired, however, when the bullet missed the insect and ricocheted off a rock, hitting the gun owner in the head and fracturing his skull.

The man survived and also learned a valuable lesson: Don't use a rifle to go after a tiny bug. Next time use a hand grenade.

Next Year They'll Be Required to Install a Central Heating System

You've read about the Ice Hotel in Sweden in almost every trivia book you've ever seen.

Located in the far northern part of the country, it is completely rebuilt every year from slabs of ice cut from the Torne river.

As unlikely as a hotel built entirely of water seems, the new regulation being imposed on it by the National Housing Board is even more unusual- the hotel is now required to have a fire alarm system!

Yes, even in a place where every wall, ceiling and floor is an automatic sprinkler system, they now need alarms.

If a fire ever did manage to break out, you wouldn't need an alarm, you'd need a snorkel!

We're not going to give up on destroying the health care system for the American people.

-Representative Paul Ryan

Patently Ridiculous

They're all invented and despite being a
bit demented they've gotten the nod from
the Patent Office...

Nokia has filed with the US Patent Office for a
new type of tattoo that may vibrate to alert you to
a phone call, remind you about your anniversary
or warn you when your battery is low. Just watch
out that your body art doesn't also needle you
when you're behind on your wireless bill.

•

Clocky is the wakeup call you can't ignore. With
Clocky, there's no negotiating. No snooze button
to buy you a few more minutes of sack time. In
fact, after Clocky goes off, it scurries away and
hides, continuing his screeching and whining beep
until you get up, track him down and finally
disarm him. Invented by a graduate of M.I.T,
Clocky is the ultimate bugle call for sleepyheads.

I am for the death penalty. Whoever commits
terrible acts must get a fitting punishment.
That way he learns the lesson for the next time.

-Britney Spears

Though patented in 1979, the 12 Gauge Golf Club has yet to catch on in a big way. That's right- whatever you shoot, you can shoot better with this explosive laden club that has a firing pin conveniently located in the sweet spot. Golfers, now your club can be as loaded as you are. It's a good thing that when Tiger Woods' ex-wife was teed off she didn't take one of these babies to him!

•

Hunters use a shooting rest to steady their aim so why not apply the same principle to urinals in men's rooms? You're probably saying, "It's so simple. Why didn't I think of that?" Well, that's why you're not a big-time inventor. This is basically a forehead rest for someone using a urinal, which provides them with support, comfort and hopefully, more accuracy.

•

There's no fun in an adult needing to wear a diaper but that doesn't mean you can't be stylish. Introducing the thong diaper, the newest craze sweeping Ipanema rest homes. This fashionable Euro-cut diaper is a must with the jet set whenever they're between continence. Invented in 2007, the thong diaper is for those who want to be ready for their next booty call even if they don't get to answer it quite in time.

Bathroom Blooper

Rear End Collision

A San Antonio woman probably wished she had a seatbelt on her commode when a car crashed into her home at a high speed and threw her off her porcelain perch. She wasn't injured but the Ty-D-Bol man was knocked overboard and has never been seen again.

Prison Suit

A convict in Oregon was fed up with conditions at the Lane County jail. Did he go on a hunger strike to draw attention to the prisoners' plight? Did he use his time to write a reasoned denunciation railing against the inhumanity of the penal system? No, he sued for $800,000.

The prison, he complained, was uncomfortable. The inmates were denied soft beds, decent food and the annual *Sports Illustrated* Swimsuit Edition. Guess there weren't any mints on the pillows or turn-down service either.

The judge dismissed his suit but despite the loss, the convict found a happy ending. He was transferred to the Snake Canyon correctional facility, where it is hoped he'll find the accommodations more to his liking.

These Pencils Really Were #2

The devil is in the details. That's what a New York City bureaucrat forgot when the city distributed thousands of public service announcement pencils.

The message was "Too cool to do drugs," a laudable sentiment indeed.

What the well-meaning bureaucrats overlooked was that there were two ways to print the message: from point to eraser and from eraser to point. They chose poorly.

"Too cool to do drugs" got shorter as the pencils were sharpened, eventually conveying the exact opposite message from what was intended.

By the time they realized their mistake, the writing was on the wall- just another example of government officials needing to get the lead out.

No, no I didn't go to England,
I went to London.

-Paris Hilton

A Tale of Two Tails

This was a story bound to have a hairy end one way or the other.

The *Express-Times* of New Jersey reported that a 23-year-old Great Meadows man allegedly slashed his 21-year-old buddy's face after they got into a heated argument over which one had the hairier rear end.

The victim was taken to a local hospital where he was stitched and treated for wounds to the face, ear and neck before being released.

The assailant was charged with aggravated assault after several witnesses on the scene helped the police get to the bottom of things.

Mixed Up Mugs

The police in North Attleboro, MA, arrested a man for passing a bogus $100 bill. The tipoff that it was counterfeit: Lincoln's mug was on the Franklin.

A man I'm proud to call my friend.
A man who will be the next president of the United States- Barack America!

-Joe Biden, at the first presidential campaign rally with Barack Obama

The "Master" Race

New research shows that Hitler was obsessed with the idea of enlisting man's best friend into the Nazi war machine.

Believing that dogs were almost as intelligent as humans, he ordered pooches recruited from all over the Fatherland to be trained in reading, tapping out messages and even speaking.

According to a report in The Telegraph, one dog was even taught to bark out "Mein Fuhrer" when asked who Hitler was- although he probably fell on his face if he tried to give the Nazi salute.

Not the Apple of Her Eye

A 9-year-old girl wrote a sweet and slightly playful letter to Apple about her devotion to her Ipod Nano. She said she wished she could dress it in a tuxedo and marry it. Like any potential wife, she also included a list of ideas to make it better.

That was too much for the legal worms at Apple. For her trouble, she received a nasty cease and desist notice for sending unsolicited ideas.

If she wasn't such an innocent child, she might have written them back with a new suggestion of exactly what they could do with their Nano.

Legal Lulus

Hundreds of thousands of new laws are
passed every year in the United States and only very
few are ever repealed. This means not only is
Justice blind, she's grossly overweight.
Here are some of the sillier statutes still on the books...

In Charlotte, North Carolina, women must have
their bodies covered in 16 yards of cloth at all
times. Beach season there must be a drag.

•

In Boise, Idaho, residents are prohibited from
fishing from a giraffe's back. Guess the only long
neck allowed on a fishing trip there is a beer.

•

In Illinois, a woman out in public on a date must
refer to the man as "Master." There is no such
requirement for married couples although many
women can be heard referring to their husbands
by a similar sounding term.

•

In New Jersey, it is illegal to slurp soup, an odd
rule to have in the home state of Campbell's.

•

In Zion, Illinois, it is against the law to give a cat,
dog or any other domesticated animal a lighted
cigar. What are they supposed to do? Light it
themselves?

Bexley, Ohio, has outlawed slot machines in outhouses. Insert your own joke about a certain casino dice game here.

•

In Florida, women can be fined for sleeping under a hair dryer. As they say, "You snooze, you lose."

•

In Chicago, it is illegal to take a French Poodle to the opera. No French Poodles? You think a schnauzer is going to appreciate culture?

•

In Florida, it is illegal for unmarried women to parachute on Sunday. It's easy to beat the law, however. If you jump from a plane and spot cops on the ground remember, you're not technically parachuting if you don't pull the ripcord.

•

In Portland, Maine, be warned: tickle a woman under the chin with a feather duster, go to jail.

•

Gary, Indiana, prohibits you from going to the theater within 4 hours of eating garlic. Anything should be prohibited within 4 hours of eating garlic!

If I die before my cat, I want a little of my ashes put in his food so I can live inside him.

-Drew Barrymore

Trial Talk

Disorder in the court is the order of the day here
in these hilarious, real courtroom exchanges.

Defendant: Judge, I want you to appoint me
another lawyer.
Judge: And why is that?
Defendant: Because the Public Defender isn't
interested in my case.
Judge (to Public Defender): Do you have any
comments on the defendant's motion?
Public Defender: I'm sorry, your Honor. I wasn't
listening.

Judge: I know you, don't I?
Defendant: Uh, yes.
Judge: All right, tell me. How do I know you?
Defendant: Judge, do I have to tell you?
Judge: Of course! You might be obstructing jus-
tice not to tell me.
Defendant: Okay. I was your bookie.

Q: What gear were you in at the moment of the
impact?
A: Gucci sweats and Reeboks.

I have determined that there is no
market for talking pictures.

-Thomas A. Edison

Bathroom Blooper

Case of the Pilfered Potty

Acton, Massachusetts, police responded to an oddball report and found that someone had indeed stolen a woman's entire bathroom. The toilet, sink, bathtub and fixtures were gone and the place was cleaned up. Investigation revealed that neighbors had seen a work truck with "Image Tile" parked outside. When they checked, it seems workers had gone to the wrong address and realized their mistake only after tearing out the bathroom, so they tidied up and left. The company offered the woman a new bathroom free of charge.

Witness Fingers Man For Crime

A 19-year-old Daytona Beach man attempted to hold up a store with his finger. When the clerk laughed, he insisted that he was serious and upped the ante by cocking his thumb and demanding money.

After determining that the finger wasn't loaded, the clerk drew his New York Finger and seeing that he was outgunned, the perp made a run for it.

A short while later the robber was apprehended and was found to be carrying 10 fingers, none of them registered.

The Sports Pages

Turning Red

In the middle of a 2004 Brazilian soccer match,
a referee reached into his pocket to pull out a red
card to eject a player. Instead, he pulled out a pair
of red panties. With a face to match the dainties,
the ref said he had no idea how the undergarment
got there, but was so embarrassed that he called
off the rest of the game.

Bird's the Word

While it's not all that unusual for a baseball card
to be printed with an error, there was one
instance in particular in which the manufacturer
was understandably embarrassed. The card was a
1989 Fleer Billy Ripken. Pictured in his Baltimore
Orioles uniform, Ripken's bat was perched over
his right shoulder with the bottom of the knob
visible. The original version was printed with an
expletive that had been written on the knob.

When the error was found, Fleer rushed to
correct it, resulting in variations of the card being
covered with marker, brushed with whiteout, and
airbrushed. Needless to say, the uncensored card
remains the most sought after version.

Derby Downer

The 1957 Kentucky Derby saw one of the biggest blunders in horseracing history.

English-bred Gallant Man, jockeyed by the legendary Willie Shoemaker, held a comfortable lead nearing the homestretch. Shoemaker, however, mistook the 16th pole for the finish line and momentarily stood up in his saddle. His unfortunate action allowed jockey Willie Hartack and his horse, Iron Liege, to close the gap and overtake Gallant Man. While Shoemaker quickly resumed driving his mount, Gallant Man was unable to catch Iron Liege. He lost by a nose.

Before the race, Gallant Man owner Ralph Lowe told the Churchill Downs track superintendents about a dream he had the previous night. Lowe explained how his jockey "stood up in the stirrups" on the colt. Sure enough, that nightmare became reality.

I don't think there's anybody in this organization not focused on the 49ers— I mean Chargers.

-Bill Belichick

The Blunderful Broadcaster

After his baseball playing career, Jerry Coleman (1924-2014) became even more well-known for his malaprops as the long-time play-by-play man of the San Diego Padres. Here's some of his best work.

• Hi folks, I'm Johnny Grubb. No I'm not. This is Jerry Coleman.

• Benedict may not be hurt as much as he really is.

• He (Graig Nettles) leaped up to make one of those diving stops only he can make.

• Ozzie Smith just made another play that I've never seen anyone else make before, and I've seen him make it more than anyone else ever has.

• Winfield goes back to the wall, he hits his head on the wall and it rolls off! It's rolling all the way back to second base. This is a terrible thing for the Padres.

• Rich Folkers is throwing up in the bullpen.

I feel like I'm the best, but you're never going to get me to say that.

-Jerry Rice

• And Kansas City is at Chicago tonight, or is that Chicago at Kansas City? Well, no matter, Kansas City leads in the eighth, four to four.

• Next up is Fernando Gonzalez, who is not playing tonight.

• There's a hard shot to LeMaster, and he throws Madlock into the dugout.

• McCovey swings and misses, and it's fouled back.

• Larry Lintz steals second standing up. He slid, but he didn't have to.

• The new Haitian baseball can't weigh more than four ounces or less than five.

• The ex-left-hander Dave Roberts will be going for Houston.

• Hector Torrez, how can you communicate with Enzo Hernandez when he speaks Spanish and you speak Mexican?

• The Phillies beat the Cubs today in the doubleheader. That puts another keg in the Cubs' coffin.

• I've made a couple of mistakes I'd like to do over.

Hot Corner Potato

In a 1980s minor league baseball game,
Williamsport hosted Reading. With an act that
could've been drawn up in the schoolyard,
perhaps it was fitting that the game's memorable
moment occurred in the same city as the Little
League World Series.

With a Reading runner on third, Williamsport
catcher Dave Bresnahan had a trick up his sleeve.
Actually, it was in his catcher's mitt. There,
Bresnahan kept a potato hidden. After a pitch, he
grabbed the potato and purposely threw it wildly
toward third base. The runner, believing it was the
baseball, trotted home. When he arrived there,
Bresnahan greeted him with the baseball he was
still holding.

The umpire, not amused, called the runner safe.
Bresnahan's bosses weren't amused either. The
next day, he was let go.

The Hall of Lame

Northern Illinois defensive end James Eggink
was a fifth round draft pick of of the Montreal
Alouettes in the 1996 Canadian Football League
Draft. The problem? He died in December 1995.

Rerun Rage

24-year-old Bryan Allison suffered multiple injuries in 2001 when he fell to the ground while throwing a 25-inch TV set off the second-floor porch of his home in Niagara Falls, N.Y., after watching a video of a 1989 hockey playoff game. He and his brother tossed the TV when they became upset over the outcome, which was presumably the same result as twelve years earlier.

A Rose is a Rose

September 11, 2010, marked the 25th anniversary of Pete Rose breaking Ty Cobb's all-time record for hits. However, the Reds, who received clearance to honor Rose despite his lifetime baseball ban for betting, had to move the celebration to a day later.

Why? Rose was making an appearance at an Indiana casino.

If you don't know where you are going,
you might wind up someplace else.

-Yogi Berra

Knock Yourself Out

Boxer Daniel Caruso was getting psyched for a 1992 Golden Gloves bout in New York, pounding his gloves into his face just before the bell rang. He accidentally rang his own bell. Caruso punched himself in the nose, bloodying and breaking it. Doctors stopped the bout before it began.

Spellbinding Notes

• The NBA's Minnesota Timberwolves handed out posters with their nickname spelled W-O-V-E-S on "Reading to Succeed Night" at the Target Center in Minneapolis.

• During a World Series broadcast, network commentator Tim McCarver proclaimed, "It's a five-letter word- S-T-R-I-K-E."

• At Florida's Derby Lane greyhound track, there was a dog named Cilohocla. The origin of the dog's name remained a mystery until someone thought to reverse the spelling.

> I may be dumb, but I'm not stupid.
>
> -Terry Bradshaw

There is No Joy in Friendsville

From 1967 to 1973, Tennessee's Friendsville Academy high school basketball team chalked up a national record 138 consecutive losses. They lost one game 71 to 0 but another only 2 to 0 when the winning basket was scored by a Friendsville player who shot the ball into the wrong hoop.

In 1970, the coach named one player--a player who had never scored a single point--the team's MVP. When reporter Douglas S. Looney from the *National Observer* questioned the coach, he tersely replied, "You don't think scoring is everything, do you?"

The conversation continued with the reporter asking, "Is there anything this team does well?"

"Not really," replied the coach.

"Are you making progress?"

"I couldn't truthfully say that we are."

"Do you like coaching?"

"I don't care that much for basketball."

The Babe's Greatest Hit

Babe Ruth may get the credit he deserves as a baseball player, but not his due as a practical joker. Bill Werber, Ruth's Yankee teammate, recounts perhaps the Bambino's most polarizing prank.

Ruth's victim was Ed Wells, a former Tigers pitcher who joined the Yanks in 1929. Following a game in Detroit, Ruth had Wells join him for a double date that evening. He told Wells that the girls loved to drink and that Wells was to supply a fifth of gin while Ruth bought a bag of oranges for a mix.

When they arrived at the suburban home, it wasn't the two ladies who greeted them at the door. Rather, it was a furious man, who yelled, "So you're the scum who's been after my wife. I oughtta kill ya!" With that, the man pulled out a snub-nosed pistol and fired at Ruth.

"I'm hit Ed!" Babe screamed, collapsing onto the porch. "Run, run for your life!"

Wells bolted from the scene, fully expecting not to make it out alive. Nevertheless, he managed to make it all the way back to the Book Cadillac Hotel where the Yankees were staying on their road trip.

At the hotel, he was greeted by grim-faced teammates in the lobby. Tony Lazzeri told Wells, "Babe's been shot. He's in bad shape and has been asking for you."

Wells was taken to Ruth's room, where the Babe was laid out in bed with talcum powder covering his face and ketchup adorning his white shirt. "He's dying, Ed," Earl Combs sobbed.

Wells passed out on the scene, but the thunder of laughter that followed quickly revived him. According to Werber, "even later we never could persuade Ed of the humor in the situation."

Bowling With Barry

You might remember when then candidate Barack Obama bowled a 37 at a Pennsylvania campaign stop in 2008. Very misleading- that was achieved in just seven frames. At that rate, the future U.S. President's score for an entire game would have been a much more respectable 53.

We're going to turn this team around 360 degrees.

-Jason Kidd

Loveable Losers

In their inaugural year, the 1962 New York Mets set a mark for the worst won-loss record in baseball history, 40-120. One incident in one game typified their futility.

The "Amazing" Mets were playing the Chicago Cubs at the Polo Grounds. "Marvelous" Marv Throneberry had just slammed a two-run triple and was standing on third when Chicago first baseman Ernie Banks called for the ball to appeal that Marv had missed first base. The appeal was upheld and Throneberry was called out.

Mets manager Casey Stengel ran out from the dugout to argue the call only to be waved off by veteran umpire Dusty Boggess who said, "Forget it, Casey. He didn't touch second either!"

He's a guy who gets up at six o'clock in the morning regardless of what time it is.

-Lou Duva, boxing trainer, on Andrew Golata